F**k This S**t:

a venting journal

What This Book is About

By now, we're all aware of the fact that we're supposed to "think positively" all the time, that "our inner worlds create our outer worlds," and that we'll be happier if we just think happy thoughts all the time. That's super great if you're a naturally happy person or if your life is perfect, but it doesn't leave a heck of a lot of space for you to actually feel some negative feelings.

Negative feelings, remember those? The ones that are supposed to be toxic to your soul, because "what you focus on grows and expands and becomes your reality"? The feelings you've been trying to squelch down since the rise of the positive psychology movement?

Here's a thought—what if you just aired those feelings out? What if, instead of trying to just "think a happy thought," you really just sat down and got all of those angry and negative thoughts out of your system?

All we're saying is, if you sit on those negative feelings and try to ignore them, they are just going to fester. If you use this journal to take them as far as they want to go, you'll get them all out and then you can move on.

Here are some examples of the categories of rants and horrible thoughts some of our readers have written about, as well as the general topics they fall under. Please feel free to refer back to them as writing prompts if you feel stuck.

All we're saying is, if you sit on those negative feelings and try to ignore them, they are just going to fester. If you use this journal to take them as far as they want to go, you'll get them

Here are some examples of the categories of rants and horrible thoughts some of our readers have written about, as well as the general topics they fall under. Please feel free to refer back to them as writing prompts if you feel stuck.

PEOPLE: People on social media, in general, especially idiotic people with loudmouth opinions. As a side note, why do these people always have the absolute worst grammar?   Could also include strangers that talk on their cellphones on speakerphone in public. Just....why?

FAMILY: Family members who you have to be nice to, even though they push you to your absolute limit. Another title for this entry might be "There better be enough booze in the house to get me through the holidays."

CAREER: Co-workers or competitors who are inexplicably more successful than you, despite the fact that you KNOW you are smarter/ more talented/ harder working than they are.

Are they using witchcraft? What do they have that you don't have?

LIFE: Why does it seem to be so difficult for a regular, hard-working person to get a decent house and raise a family? Isn't this the "American dream"? How is this possible anymore, when you are killing yourself at work and still living in an overpriced apartment/ rental house?

HEALTH: Some of the nicest people you know end up getting terrible diseases and dying, while inconsiderate a-holes are in perfect health. Discuss.

NEIGHBORS: especially neighbors who have no concept of disturbing other people. This includes, but is most certainly not limited to: people who play their terrible music too loud, people who let their dogs bark for hours on end, people with loud children who seem to want the neighborhood to babysit for them, and people with loud cars.

WEIGHT: That's where you eat a carrot stick every day and gain four pounds, while your annoying friends and co-workers weigh 100 pounds and complain about how fat they think they are, OR (perhaps even worse) say things on social media like "Oh yeah...I can eat whatever I want and I never gain weight!" when you know full well they have an eating disorder. Fuck them.

KIDS: you are supposed to love them and take care of them, so why are they such jerks? Did you really sign up to be a chauffer and a short- order cook? Where do these kids get off being so entitled?

ADULTING : did it not seem like being an adult was going to be MUCH more awesome than it actually is? Someone really should have warned us about the pressure of huge decisions, and financial burdens, and crying in your car.

OTHER: Including, but not limited to, insurance companies whose whole business is just to not pay your claims, companies that are dying to slap you with huge late fees and ruin your life if you miss your bill's due date by five minutes, and your cellphone provider in general.

Pick a topic:

PEOPLE   HEALTH

FAMILY   CAREER   LIFE

NEIGHBORS   WEIGHT

KIDS   ADULTING

OTHER

Get it all out:

_____

_____

_____

_____

_____

_____

_____

_____

_____

_____

Pick a topic:

PEOPLE   HEALTH

FAMILY   CAREER   LIFE

NEIGHBORS   WEIGHT

KIDS   ADULTING

OTHER

Get it all out:

_____

_____

_____

_____

_____

_____

_____

_____

_____

_____

_____

Pick a topic:

PEOPLE   HEALTH

FAMILY   CAREER   LIFE

NEIGHBORS   WEIGHT

KIDS   ADULTING

OTHER

Get it all out:

_____

_____

_____

_____

_____

_____

_____

_____

_____

_____

Pick a topic:

PEOPLE   HEALTH

FAMILY   CAREER   LIFE

NEIGHBORS   WEIGHT

KIDS   ADULTING

OTHER

Get it all out:

_____

_____

_____

_____

_____

_____

_____

_____

_____

_____

_____

Pick a topic:

PEOPLE   HEALTH

FAMILY   CAREER   LIFE

NEIGHBORS   WEIGHT

KIDS   ADULTING

OTHER

Get it all out:

_____

_____

_____

_____

_____

_____

_____

_____

_____

_____

_____

Pick a topic:

PEOPLE   HEALTH

FAMILY   CAREER   LIFE

NEIGHBORS   WEIGHT

KIDS   ADULTING

OTHER

Get it all out:

_____

_____

_____

_____

_____

_____

_____

_____

_____

_____

Pick a topic:

PEOPLE   HEALTH

FAMILY   CAREER   LIFE

NEIGHBORS   WEIGHT

KIDS   ADULTING

OTHER

Get it all out:

_____

_____

_____

_____

_____

_____

_____

_____

_____

_____

_____

_____

Pick a topic:

PEOPLE   HEALTH

FAMILY   CAREER   LIFE

NEIGHBORS   WEIGHT

KIDS   ADULTING

OTHER

Get it all out:

_____

_____

_____

_____

_____

_____

_____

_____

_____

_____

_____

Pick a topic:

PEOPLE   **HEALTH**

FAMILY   **CAREER**   **LIFE**

NEIGHBORS   **WEIGHT**

KIDS   **ADULTING**

OTHER

Get it all out:

_____

_____

_____

_____

_____

_____

_____

_____

_____

_____

Pick a topic:

PEOPLE   HEALTH

FAMILY   CAREER   LIFE

NEIGHBORS   WEIGHT

KIDS   ADULTING

OTHER

Get it all out:

_____

_____

_____

_____

_____

_____

_____

_____

_____

Pick a topic:

PEOPLE   HEALTH

FAMILY   CAREER   LIFE

NEIGHBORS   WEIGHT

KIDS   ADULTING

OTHER

Get it all out:

_____

_____

_____

_____

_____

_____

_____

_____

_____

Pick a topic:

PEOPLE   HEALTH

FAMILY   CAREER   LIFE

NEIGHBORS   WEIGHT

KIDS   ADULTING

OTHER

Get it all out:

_____

_____

_____

_____

_____

_____

_____

_____

_____

_____

Pick a topic:

PEOPLE   **HEALTH**

FAMILY   **CAREER**   **LIFE**

NEIGHBORS   **WEIGHT**

KIDS   **ADULTING**

OTHER

Get it all out:

_____

_____

_____

_____

_____

_____

_____

_____

_____

_____

_____

Pick a topic:

PEOPLE   HEALTH

FAMILY   CAREER   LIFE

NEIGHBORS   WEIGHT

KIDS   ADULTING

OTHER

Get it all out:

_____

_____

_____

_____

_____

_____

_____

_____

_____

_____

Pick a topic:

PEOPLE   HEALTH

FAMILY   CAREER   LIFE

NEIGHBORS   WEIGHT

KIDS   ADULTING

OTHER

Get it all out:

_____

_____

_____

_____

_____

_____

_____

_____

_____

_____

_____

_____

_____

Pick a topic:

PEOPLE   HEALTH

FAMILY   CAREER   LIFE

NEIGHBORS   WEIGHT

KIDS   ADULTING

OTHER

Get it all out:

_____

_____

_____

_____

_____

_____

_____

_____

_____

_____

Pick a topic:

PEOPLE   **HEALTH**

FAMILY   **CAREER**   **LIFE**

NEIGHBORS   **WEIGHT**

KIDS   **ADULTING**

OTHER

Get it all out:

_____

_____

_____

_____

_____

_____

_____

_____

_____

_____

Pick a topic:

PEOPLE   HEALTH

FAMILY   CAREER   LIFE

NEIGHBORS   WEIGHT

KIDS   ADULTING

OTHER

Get it all out:

_____

_____

_____

_____

_____

_____

_____

_____

_____

_____

_____

Pick a topic:

PEOPLE   HEALTH

FAMILY   CAREER   LIFE

NEIGHBORS   WEIGHT

KIDS   ADULTING

OTHER

Get it all out:

_____

_____

_____

_____

_____

_____

_____

_____

_____

_____

Pick a topic:

PEOPLE   HEALTH

FAMILY   CAREER   LIFE

NEIGHBORS   WEIGHT

KIDS   ADULTING

OTHER

Get it all out:

Pick a topic:

PEOPLE   **HEALTH**

FAMILY   **CAREER**   **LIFE**

NEIGHBORS   **WEIGHT**

KIDS   **ADULTING**

OTHER

Get it all out:

Pick a topic:

PEOPLE   HEALTH

FAMILY   CAREER   LIFE

NEIGHBORS   WEIGHT

KIDS   ADULTING

OTHER

Get it all out:

_____

_____

_____

_____

_____

_____

_____

_____

_____

_____

Pick a topic:

PEOPLE   HEALTH

FAMILY   CAREER   LIFE

NEIGHBORS   WEIGHT

KIDS   ADULTING

OTHER

Get it all out:

_____

_____

_____

_____

_____

_____

_____

_____

_____

_____

Pick a topic:

PEOPLE   HEALTH

FAMILY   CAREER   LIFE

NEIGHBORS   WEIGHT

KIDS   ADULTING

OTHER

Get it all out:

_____

_____

_____

_____

_____

_____

_____

_____

_____

_____

_____

Pick a topic:

PEOPLE   HEALTH

FAMILY   CAREER   LIFE

NEIGHBORS   WEIGHT

KIDS   ADULTING

OTHER

Get it all out:

_____

_____

_____

_____

_____

_____

_____

_____

_____

_____

_____

Pick a topic:

PEOPLE   HEALTH

FAMILY   CAREER   LIFE

NEIGHBORS   WEIGHT

KIDS   ADULTING

OTHER

Get it all out:

_____

_____

_____

_____

_____

_____

_____

_____

_____

_____

Pick a topic:

PEOPLE   HEALTH

FAMILY   CAREER   LIFE

NEIGHBORS   WEIGHT

KIDS   ADULTING

OTHER

Get it all out:

_____

_____

_____

_____

_____

_____

_____

_____

_____

_____

Pick a topic:

PEOPLE   HEALTH

FAMILY   CAREER   LIFE

NEIGHBORS   WEIGHT

KIDS   ADULTING

OTHER

Get it all out:

_____

_____

_____

_____

_____

_____

_____

_____

_____

_____

Pick a topic:

PEOPLE   HEALTH

FAMILY   CAREER   LIFE

NEIGHBORS   WEIGHT

KIDS   ADULTING

OTHER

Get it all out:

_____

_____

_____

_____

_____

_____

_____

_____

_____

_____

_____

Pick a topic:

PEOPLE   HEALTH

FAMILY   CAREER   LIFE

NEIGHBORS   WEIGHT

KIDS   ADULTING

OTHER

Get it all out:

_____

_____

_____

_____

_____

_____

_____

_____

_____

_____

Pick a topic:

PEOPLE   **HEALTH**

FAMILY   **CAREER**   **LIFE**

NEIGHBORS   **WEIGHT**

KIDS   **ADULTING**

OTHER

Get it all out:

Pick a topic:

PEOPLE   HEALTH

FAMILY   CAREER   LIFE

NEIGHBORS   WEIGHT

KIDS   ADULTING

OTHER

Get it all out:

_____

_____

_____

_____

_____

_____

_____

_____

_____

_____

_____

Pick a topic:

PEOPLE   HEALTH

FAMILY   CAREER   LIFE

NEIGHBORS   WEIGHT

KIDS   ADULTING

OTHER

Get it all out:

_____

_____

_____

_____

_____

_____

_____

_____

_____

_____

_____

_____

_____

_____

Pick a topic:

PEOPLE   HEALTH

FAMILY   CAREER   LIFE

NEIGHBORS   WEIGHT

KIDS   ADULTING

OTHER

Get it all out:

_____

_____

_____

_____

_____

_____

_____

_____

_____

_____

_____

_____

Free Gift

This is an actual game that we developed during the pandemic. We've played it every Saturday night for the past two years, so we know it works online. We've also played it in person, and it is just as funny.

https://funnystrangepress.com/game

Made in United States
Orlando, FL
13 December 2022

26440180R10078